Putting together the piec

written by

alycia marie rosenberg

PUTTING TOGETHER THE PIECES

First edition. March 3, 2024.

ISBN: 979-8224199174

Written by Alycia marie rosenberg.

Table of Contents

Address
Phone
E-mail

•

Putting together the pieces:
Tips for parents with kids with behavior problems

As an individual with ADHD, I know first hand the challenges encountered by children faced with this disorder. I am writing this for parents and teachers to gain knowledge from someone that has ADHD. I want parents and caregivers to know there is hope for their child. In writing this book i realized many things. The first was there is always hope. Children with behavior issues are very special chldren. If the children can get the help they need early on alot can be changed. That is the second thing I learned in the research is that with help and early intervention a child will succed. Early intevention is possible . Change is possible. It has to be or a generation of children will be lost. I know. I was the child from a very young age that was picked on. They did not know know as much as they know now. As much progress as they have made with children with behavior problems due to ADHD and autism there still is more work that needs to be done. I am writing this to give parents hope. Further This will be a guide of where parents can go to get their child the help to succeed in life and beyond. I am writing this further for the little girl I once was and the woman I now am.

Highschool years :
Thoughts of a adhd /autism girl
Me 1992
Volleyball hater,Speggettie eating,
Actress,writer,With hazel eyes,
Playing softball,Playing the guitar,
Critizing finger nail tappers,
Walking fast,Talking a lot,
Brownish black hair, Wearing glasses,
Like a bee going from flower to flower,
Like a cat cuddling with loved ones,
Complicted as a computer,
Wearing pink,unsure of how I look,

Afraid of dying,
A love for and honoring Jesse Jackson,
Hoping someday to be called star,
White on the outside, Many colors on the inside,
Knowing all the questions,
Unsure of the answers to the questions.

MY INITIATION 11 15 93

How appropriate that I bleed? On the day I was born, I enter my young adulthood the same way that I came into the world. I now know why some say blood is perfect for initiation. The brightness of the color oozing out says I'm here. Blood is healthy not dirty. I know that now covered with blood. I entered the world now I look and see the blood flowing how appropriate today Leave behindThe world I knew so well and come into a world just as exciting but one I know not as well looking down. I see the redness and know that I am blessed on this day.

3 7 91 Threw a child's eyes

The child sits and listens to the older ones. They seem so why she thinks. In such big words, she starts to yawn, and the Mommy comes and picks her up and carries her to bed such big hands and she walked so fast and my guess the bed is so big. I hear what I hope. I don't get lost tonight when i'm asleep.

The search 3 7 91

The child wanders from place to place searching for something. She feels that she has lost though. She knows not what it is. She wanders on and on. But cannot remember what it is that she has lost so on and on. She goes never resting always Searching For this unknown object soon she will find it and then she will stop searching. She must continue searching for only when she stops. Will she find what she is looking for is herself.

1991 mommy

I hug my daughter and cry enter a shoulder. My tears aren't really tears but just memories flowing from my eyes. I'm looking to my daughter's eyes and see a young woman starting out.

Here we stand 1991

Here we stand holding hands. We have no faces age or color together. We stand in the darkness link together like a chain in the darkness. We are like sisters guiding and supporting each other in the dark. We don't harass or name call we're loving and caring. Another vietnamtroubled times

Nov 2nd 1990

The year was 1990. The month was August. Kids were getting ready.

Kids were getting bored, parents and anxious for school to open when it happened when what happened when world peace was shattered. When our boys and girls were shipped overseas. I was coming back for the movies. When they stopped to glance at the papers. I saw the headlines. I crunched on the ground to read it. Having finished I stood up and walked on wondering why this was happening. My gayety was gone. My walk was heavy and my heart was crying the next day. I saw another paper which said. Saddam Hussein chemical weapons not afraid to use them. I went home to my bed and cried for weeks. I watched the news and red papers. The government said. Don't worry, we'll handle it. I watched as the situation grew worse. It started with them holding Americans and it became a thing of Pride. It was like they were children playing kids games only. It wasn't, and they weren't the government kept saying. Hey, it's okay, people are laughing in the check. Outlines. Are people are making it seem like summer camp? I was confused upset and sad. Why now? I asked? I wish I'm stars for this to be over. I cry myself. To sleep wondering, will I wake up? Every day I do and every day, I ask what next. I hear people whispering in corners about how crazy Hussain is. I wonder though I mean, is it him or is it us? Do we have a right to be there or are we invading? I avoid the papers now and I don't watch the news anymore. I try to not to listen to the talk about everywhere I go but everywhere I go. People are saying what if when we go I shudder at those words. And block them out. I cry a lot not on the outside, but inside the crying is eating at me and leaving me scared. Will this be another Vietnam? Will we go uninvited? With people yell, bring our boys home only now. What about girls? We'll be another Vietnam or even worse. And if it is at least in vietnam , they had a home to come back to.

End of the run

Tears fall life is back to normal boring again. But something will turn up life again will be, but till then I can

breathe again and then it will start all over. I like it when it's out of control and I can't breathe. It's so exciting. Beginnings are never are nerve-racking. Middle school middles are fat and endings are sad , but the best is knowing the people in knowing the process and that it will start all over again when it ends the endingThis means happy sad and everything in between.

11 191 glory day

A soldier's glory is not on the battlefield But on a street in a parade. On a day called Veterans Day a day meant to show soldiers. We love them and respect you and that we are proud of them for keeping the old red white and blue flying high.

11 3 92 election day

The people knew what they wanted and got it. Hip hip hip hooray, 3 Cheers for the President. He is our man. He'll change the world. He'll make America strong how even renew the American dream. We love you, Clinton, hail Clinton. The true leader he is strong and mighty. And he is ours long live clinton and the american people.

11 3 92 a new world

The first Native American, an African American in the senate, a President with no military experience, a working woman in the White House. A child in the White House, not since Kennedy. Did things look so good a good v? P? The American people are talking taking back their government.Everything is changing no longer. Will the world be messed up... We are coming together and we will create a better world. The racism will diminish and we will stand together like Martin. Luther king junior so long ago promised. The poor will no longer be poor and the rich will no longer be rich. Everyone will be equal for the first time in history.

Snow flakes

Snowflakes are like candy only better snowflakes are like art. No 2 are the same. Everyone has a different and unique shape. They fall as millions, but become one when they hit the ground. But each are still keeping their own identity just like you and me.

What summer means to me

Summer is when Baby Animals see the world. Summer is a time to roam free? Summer is a time to plant a garden summer is a lovely time of year.

The summer sun

The summer sun nourishes the ground and gives it energy for the rest of the year. The sun of the summer gives the animal's energy for the rest of the year. It makes plants grow and it gives humans energy to live. The summer sun nourishes and gives life to all never asking for anything in return.

Click your heals thrice

Oh, how I await the cold snowy days for when it gets cold. Then soon I will be leaving this place that I am bored too. And going to the place that I call home the place that my heart craves . A home, we'll go when the cold snowy days come ,oh how my heart does long for the long snowy days that will take me back home to my mama and my little baby brother. I love them so and I long for the day that the snow will blow me home to the coziest place to ever be a home again home again. I will be at the first winter snow.

New york in the summer

New York is like the desert in the hot month of this summer. You want to cool off from the heat? So you find the first puddle and soak your poor aching feet.

Eleven twenty eight ninety one

I remember the pilgrims and the Indians to some Thanksgiving is a time for lots of food and family and to others it is time to get ready for Christmas but neither of those are fully speaking the truth, Thanksgiving is the time to remember your neighbor and top others. This is the reason we celebrate Thanksgiving, so we'remember the Indians and the pilgrims and remember that if it were not for the Indians, we might not even be here today.

Eleven seventeen ninety five

Living

Around and round the world goes where it stops, nobody knows faster and faster and faster. It goes, the faster goes the dizzier. You get beg for the world to slow down, but it won't, and so you are stuck. You wish and wish, but even that doesn't work. Finally, you realize that nothing will make the world ghost slower. All you can do is live each moment to the fulleEst.

Stand tall

It is time for the people of the world to come together to not

To be afraid and to not be afraid of things that are different. It is time trying to watch the field from their minds. Is it time to step out of the dark ages? Can really look about them. It is a time to hold out your hand embrace the people of the world because we will all belong together. And until we become one, the world will be at a stand still..

What keeps you going

When I stepped outside the warming of the day embraced me. I knew it would not last and again. There would be bone chilly days, I still let the warmth embrace me and I let myself feel the magic waiting to come out. As I had thought, the warmth was gone soon but I held in my head had the warmth and the magic. That would fill the days with beauty..

mom 7 8 93

As you blow out the candles feel my presence though I am far away. Know that I'm thinking of you and wishing to be there with you. I love you and wish you all the love in the world. May your wish come true.

7 8 93 Healthy at last

Today Mommy, I truly accept who you are. I will no longer wish for a mom who calls before she goes away no today. I love you for what you are and not for what I want you to be on your birthday. I give you the best gift of all total love today I Have learned To accept you for you, oh mama, you're so special. Happy birthday to you I accept you today and evermore happy birthday.

Twilight

Twilight to me is like a giant black & white movie. Knowing no boundaries and having no screen. The best thing though about twilight is that it has more realness than any black and White movie we will ever have.

Escape

Run runaway to school to friend. Just don't go home. I run to a safe haven where the conversation is safei'm running. Yes, I'm running. I'm running to my special placethat is safe from the outside world where no danger comes in where there is no hate. Just love I am so safe. I never want to leave.

Why can't I stay in my special place forever and ever I cry? I went to my place but walked slowly home.

Teen star 59 ninety three

It is strange to see young kids going gaga over Luke Perry. I remember when it was Kirk Cameron who, who caused the commotion and decades ago, it was The Beatles, though teen stars come and go, one thing is for sure,Every generation has someone who makes them scream that causes shivers and are first crushes. They come and go today, Luke, tomorrow Who knows.no one knows who it'll be for sure But one thing is certain they will make everyone scream.

new power eleven three ninety two

The democrats are here bye bye republicans. This is the year of the Democrat, a Democrat Congress and the Democrat President. We're moving from the old ways to new ones.

This transfer of power is just what we needed for going into the new century. People went change and change is what they will get.

Eleven three ninety two super heroes and villains

The democrats are super heroes and the republicans are villains. When you need something done, call a Democrat, but watch out for the republicans who lie and cheat to get it their way. We have a super hero in office now the goddess knew We were suffering and get and gave us some good. We waited a long time and now we've got what we wanted.

Wondering of a young woman

Sometimes I wonder if I'm the only one left when I think that it leads me to another puzzling. Thought am I just abnormal or just a bit weird? I look at every guy I see and feel weird inside.Am I ugly or Or meant to be a guy. Is it weird to wonder so much? Or is it only natural for an almost woman.

12 27 92

The tears flow from my eyes. It used to be me now. It is him how How strange life is. I want to hold him and never let him go I miss him so much. The bond we shared is so deep. Seeing him go I see myself at his age. The tears I cry are for me as much as for him. I'm remembering all The Times I was sad and happy and confused hoping it is easier. For him my brother, I love you so much. It isn't easy to see you go. The house seems so empty. I keep expecting to see you. It feels as though you're only away at a friend's. But you're not. it is so hard to say Goodbye. Come home soon and make the tears stop.

Death

Death works behind bushes under beds and under dark places.

Just waiting to grab you and suck your soul out of you. If you don't want the death monster to do that to you , I have only one word of advice , be as careful as you can.

Growing up

Growing up can be scary. It can be painful too. Growing up is painful and new. There is no rule book to help you through the difficult years that you're going through. People will say they understand what you are going through. But you know that That they can not possibly understand Even if they did you would still haveEven if they did , you would still have to cope with growing up , so what doesn't matter if they understand or. not.

the run down house

I used to live in that house. The one over there with a broken down door and little mice running around on the floor the windows are dirty. There's a hole in the roof and the floors are a mess, Yes I used to live in that house in my day it was grand.

Exhaustion three seventeen ninety one

This people move slowly listening to the mother's voice as they move, empty fields, the parched ground is exhausted. They fall to the ground. Their tears fall onto the mother who has long since forgotten what falling water feels like.

Warnings

We warned you, we warned you? That your ways would catch up with you. But you would not listen to us now, You see, It does not matter. The rivers are polluted. The trees are gone and all the children are shut up in houses, soon, though you won't get used to it. Evil white man, we have warned you now you must pay.

The dance

Listen, and you shall hear the drums. We have been dancing and praying for many moons. Our bodies are growing weary and still we dance. We dance for the goddess who watches us. She will tell us when we have danced enough. She watches us in smiles as we dance we learn the true meaning of life.

Summer solstice

There's something magical about the 1st day of summer and make sure stop anotice all the beauty that surrounds you. The birds sing a little louder. The grass is greener and life is all around rosy on the first day of summer.

Spring solstice

Spring has come though. It may not seem like it to. Day. It has come and soon. We will see the beautiful things that went away when winter snows covered the ground again. Will the weather be warm and again? We shall see cute little animals roaming the world soon. The world will be warm and trees will be covered with weeds instead of snow Alas. She's back the season of Spring. The joy is season of Spring has returned. We thank you for blessing us with your presence once again.

Almighty season of change and new beginnings. You are well logged. You never forget as longlived, the mighty season of Spring .homatokweasa

Memorial day nineteen ninety

Veterans put on the brave and gettfront for us. The deep down there are scared and wanna cry. I have nothing against veteransi'll never spit or name call. I may not have a high opinion of why they do what they do but always honor them and remember what they fought for.

The little puerto rican

The little putroticrn comes out every day at 3 to see what he can see. He comes to see what is going on, but instead he gets pushed and shoved and hauled at the little puerto rican is only 7, but still they push and scream. They don't even know him but still they are mean to him. Why ask why are they so mean to the little portirican.

The snob

Whenever we see the snob, her nose is stuck high in the air. She wears the latest fads. And it's the finest food and always knows what to say. She always seems to smile. But if you look in her eyes we see she isn't as happy as she pretends to be.

Rag to riches

Someday I know my dream will come true someday. I'll have a great big house someday. I'll have a great big fancy car someday. I'll be away from here and I'll buy a great big house for my ma and pa.

Tonight 4 3 93

Oh how my body aches for your touch, you're the one I have been waiting for i can tell by the look in your eyes you love me. I thought you'd never come oh, how many nights I fell asleep dreaming I would find you tonight's the night of my dreams and I know tonight will be magic, so hug me tight and say sweet things in my ear. I waited so long to find You & I will. never let you go.

Mother earth

You see and feel her every day, but yet take her for granted. Whether it be Spring days a winter evening, a fall afternoon or summer night. You may say your beauty will always be there for you.

But that may not be true, so don't take her for granted. Appreciate her and help clean her up. Because how long can one be without the proper nourishment?.

People

People make up the world not colors races. Men, women, people make up the world. It's time to stop looking at faces and seeing a Race. It's time to stop acting like animals and start acting like the human. Time to rid ourselves of the hate . It is time to say we are all people no matter what we look like..

1 20 92

The dreamer

For those who dream, never stop dreaming. For it is only the dreamers who notice the little things the dream or makes everyday special without the dreamer. What would life be like? I shudder at the thought and hope that the dreamer never dies

Freedom for you and me

Rich and poor old and young. I'll sing the same song of freedom. The freedom song knows no boundaries and has no prejudice. So whoever you are the freedom song will always sing for you

Freedom song

The song of the freedom is sweet, is Music to your ears. Whoever you are, freedom will always be on your side. So never mind anyone talk you out of what you deserve freedom.

Snow

When it snows, you can do lots of things to name. Just a few sledding building snow people and houses not to mention skiing so I have lots of fun and don't forget to build a frosty.

Hey now come together

It's time for the people of the world to come together and to be Not afraid Of things that are different to wash the filth from their minds, it's time to come out of our darkness and really look at the people that we share the world with. It's time to seek the truth. It's time to hold out our hands and embrace the people of the world. You are the same as me and i'm the same as you.

1 21 93

The shadows

He stands in the shadows, wondering what went wrong. There is supposed to be a team working in living the Dream together.

Now it's all him he waves and they scream and I sent in the shadows waiting for my turn. Do they remember my name does it matter? This is his dream. His life and all I can do is wait together. We could have been great alone. We are nothing he will see, but then it will be too late. We are drifting, he is going up and I am waiting in the wings. Yes , he is standing in the shadows , watching waiting observing and hoping that he will get his turn.

Waiting mother's day nineteen ninety four

I sit by the phone waiting. Watching hoping I watch The Red light. Hoping to see a blink. I promise myself. I won't give in to the feelings, but oh, why? Oh, why Mamma don't you call doesn't matter? Yes, yes, my heart cries stop. Don't regress o pain, great pain, d*** you, mama. I pick up a stuff outbook and throw it down in pain. I try to forget what day it is. No I will not regret my heart closed with tears as they wonder what you were doing today..

Summer

Oh God, I hate summer. The pain of leaving everything behind. Can't everything just stay the same the tears fall down my eyes.

As I remember the child and me always coming and going to a new place to childhood, rather be in school. She hates to break the pattern. Give me strength, I must break away. It's time I must heal my child within me and thus, I will heal my grown up me. Then only then why feel no more pain?.

Crowded streets

The streets are all crowded and the houses are all empty.

Where have all the people gone? Where have all the people gone look, and you? You shall see what The government has done ,look over there on the ground. The people sleeping on the ground are the people that used to live in the houses. Now they live in the streets with no pillows and only a newspaper As a blanket, they once were solid citizens down on their lock. Now they have to beg for food and lay on the ground homeless and friendless.

Wide eyed innocent ten two ninety two

Oh, how young they look. I was never that young. Looking at the smiling face and realizing how naive they are. How I'm knowing they don't have a care in the world. They want to grow up. I silently pray for them to realize how good they have it. And before they know it, they will be gone. And they too will be looking back as I do now . Like me at their age, they are singing and grasping, for what they want and waiting .While they wait They remain wide eyed and innocent.

Wondering ten two ninety two

Oh I wonder what could have been. I might have been Jason Dee's girlfriend. I could have been popular. Gone to prom and kiss. I could have gone on things. I'll never know what i could have been. I'll always wonder what my life would be like if things have been different.In different choice made.

Mothers and daughters eleven one ninety two

Once upon a time I could sit on your lap. And you'd make everything better. It seems days are gone forever. I'm growing up and you're getting older, . Don't hold me forever. But mama sometimes I wish you could wrap me up in your arms and protect me from the world and make everything better. I remember the warmth of your hands as you pick me up. At the back how they were how you smelled and your hair I long to be wrapped in your arms for you to make everything better when I cried, you could make everything better. You would cuddle me close and say it will be OK, I grow older and I want it. Sit for hours playing. You made everything better talking on the phone I still can smell the bread mama, and how delicious it was.And I stand they're looking and smiling. And the rare occasions you would go out. You would kiss me Goodbye and I would smell your perfume. Jasmine, and they will get your kisses. As you kiss me on the cheek and you would cuddle. When you came home, I remember everything, and I wish I was that young age and you could make anything go away. As I grew older, our lives are different. We go different ways but you will always be there for me.

Sunshine

When the sun shines down on you, it warms your inner soul. It brings happines And love the sun takes pain away. It replaces shivers with smiles and let you know what love is like

Forever

The word forever is a happy word though I ask myself what it means ,to some it means , to always have one another . To high school kids a week, so asking what it means. I come up with No answer, so I leave it to you to define it for yourself. The meaning that best suits you, forever means something different to each student that roams the world.

Pioneer ghost nine fourteen ninety two

If you look, you can see the ghost of yesterday they travel by your side. And whisper in your ear, you can see them, building the rail or milking The cows ,treat them with respect and honor there presence and they will never harm you.

Hopefuls 3 5 91

The orphones line up smiling and praying today will be the day to leave. They smile brightly and stop talking as the

Mommy's and daddy's go by. But no one stops to look at them. They just walk right on by and asking where the babies are...

Nakedness

4 8 91

Now the Earth was naked. No more trees or babbling Brooks or children running freeling. All that was gone , now , all the earth could hear with the gentle swish of the wind as it went past and all she could do was wait for she knew some day that the things of earth would return and she would be naked no longer.

Birthdays

AS A BABY, PEOPLE PINCH your CHEEKS, AND
SAY HOW CUTE YOU ARE, BUT WHEN YOU GET

OLDER, NO. LONGER WILL THEY PINCHED,BUT THEY GIVE YOU CHECKS AND PUT YOU ON YOUR WAY.

Trees 4 2 92

The arms sway back-and-forth and try to grab what is there hair shakes about, his voice calls out? I want to protect you, to give you food. Provide homes,often he is mistaken for a big horrible monster, who is out for blood, but once you get a second chance, you find out that he really is as Harmless as a lamb.

4 9 91 cheerleader

She shouts and Cheers at every score .When the Final whistle blows she runs to the field and runs to a football player and gives him a Hardy hug on the field .

Football player

He grunts, he Kicks, he runs, he scores. The game is over. He is sweaty all over but he smiled at the fans and hugs his girl.

The crowd

4 14 91

When the last touchdown is made, the crowd clamps and shouts and stumps. Everyone is hugging shouting and smiling and laughing.

Changing of the guards

8 11 92

Everything is changing. You can feel the Earth moving . with Every step we are closer to change out with the old, and in with the new nothing will ever be the same again, it is time for earth to claim it's rightful heir ,It is time ,the planet is shifing the goddess has spoken. She knows what she wants, she knows what is right. The goddess is spoken and so it will be.

,

chapter one

Case study

Three years old. a female. No friends. Biting. Antisocial. Throwing fits. No Parnell play. No Scemas. Does not listen. Will not play with others. Knows under 1000 words. does not understand emotions can not tell when ome one is upset or happy. Does not know the sequance of events. Is random , even more so then normal for their age.

This is my case study. As far back as I can remember I was singled out for being different. The other children would make fun of me, starting in elementary school. I felt like I was not a part of groups. I was always behind in what was going on and took longer to understand the rules of a game. These problems lead to me feeling left behind and lost as a young child. These feelings only intensified as I got older.

Preschool through elementary school years I was barely making may way. Then elementry school happned. I was doing okay. That said my mum had to do lots of work with the teachers. My mum manged to get teachers on board. I had a few friends. All this added up to a fairly good grade school experience. I have no real problems with those years. Though as my hormones raged things got worse.

By my teen years I did not feel good about myself and learned to retreat into myself,as a coping technique to help myself not get treated badly. Retreating protected me from further getting hurt. I did activities that required the least interaction possible. I was on the school newspaper and in drama. Both activities allowed me to be a part of something but only minimally. That was fine with me. I had few friends in school.

Now later in life I struggle to maintain friendships and keep my circle of friends small. I am always asking myself if something is right or wrong. I am always watching my behavior so I do not get frustrated or upset and act out.

My behavior problems are a big part of my lack of friends. As a child I was always acting out and getting frustrated. As I grew older I distanced more from people as a way to control my behavior. By distancing from people I only managed to isolate myself. This was not the best behavior management skill. Now that I am older I am learning better behavior management skills. Further, I am not isolating from people.

The degree of intervention that I did receive as a child helped me achieve what I have thus far. Having received some early intervention I see the importance of it for preschool age children. I want to help families and children understand themselves, and their child better. I will do this by giving parents and children the support and skills they need, so there can hopefully be even fewer difficulties. While I did receive some early intervention as a child, there was more that could be done. Now though there is so much more help available to children and families.

I want to take my life experiences and use them to help children. I will use my own experiences and research to create a plan for families and teachers. I will also create ways to help children better that have ADHD and behavior management problems. I feel that my Insight and direct experiences will add something new to the field. I bring that unique experience and talk from the understanding of what a child needs and the knowledge I have. The research I find will help the preschool child receive early intervention in the classroom.

Now I a spirtspirtual life coach and stand up comic . I got my first degree in theatre. I did acting and theatre. For a few years. I realized I liked helping people and began to study psychology. I am single still and take herbs for my ADHD, changa and menopausal herbs. That medication helps me. I feel more grounded now then ever before.I feel that I am I am on the right path. I am off and running so to speak. The world is my oster. From my mum I received lots of intervention. My mum worked really hard at getting teachers to understand me early on. I think that she could do that because she knew my troubles early on.

Yes I still have mood swings. Everyday I struggle with my disabilities. Through therapy, meds, and support and many trial and error I have come to the point I am. I am not the child wondering, waiting or hoping. Like I was in 1992 in English class in Pittsburgh pa. I am a middle age women who went through the he'll of menopause and petimenspayse and had my disability gett stronger and anxiety worse.

Just like I was in high school in ninety grade before my period.Hormons raged and I was bad. We were told it would ho away but now we know more about adhd autism . .. I wrote this so people will know how to help the child early and know what to expect in teens and as a adult in peri menopause, I was the first generation to go through adhd and still the first as a middle age women. I want people to know it's not way but with counseling and you can get through it. Every generation has it easier. Today kids are called neurodiverant and walk around there class room and chew on toys . For me I had to make it up. There was no one saying walk around yes I got extra time on projects and learning writings but my anxiety was in full swing and It still surprises me that my body knew to chew on pencils which had lead but it realized my anxiety so I risked it. I know what i need and I needed to relax and chewing helps you find that zen place. Also I chewed gum and ate sour candy which helped with my anxiety all things that are coming to light. My coping skills are getting better now and finally un doing a life of anxiety and bad skills. With no place for parents to go for support and me either it was like the wild west . Just knowing what my body needed. I know I couldn't handle recess and so I stayed in. Amazing. Even then I did what I needed. Today I am finally ready as a member of the 50s club, glup, to find love and maybe kids...someone else's, that ship has sailed. Ready to wow the world with my knowledge of autism and adhd and make people laugh for playing a Jewish itilian mother. I never dated much in school but hollywoid comedys rom voms and sweet valley high sweet dreams were my exscape.Dreaming of that idea of love. And even though I didn't have faith that a guy would date me and I was a later bloomer I still dreamed of prom. I didn't go to dances no . I almost asked a guy out in ashland oregon English class but it was a sadies dance girl ask guy dance. Yes I'm that old that wad a thing. right...But I had no confidence so I did not . He moved away and after a stay in a hospital saw him once but was that .So dating was bad.but books and hollywood gave me love and a life. I closed my eyes and found what I needed. I'm finally not dreaming but living .

The question (1992)

Wondering,Waiting,Hoping,

For that special question that every teen wants to hear.Those words that means very much.Prom you and me.Oh that brings a smile to my face.

College wanderings

I hope this book can help kids today not to have just escape and for parents to find out a away to help their babies at a early age it rely works. This was my thesis in 2012 so some may be out dated but it still works. By getting kids the help they need early there will not be prison, hospitals, or broken dreams

And a life time of struggles. I was never in prison but hand cuffs enough and hospitals yes. I know it's still not rainbows and roses for everyone but I hope the right person people find this and see how to help their baby's and even adults and see wherever what yoy were missing and know you can fix it . I could and am. You can.

Enjoy the book and my comedy I'm including about dating with adhd and life with adhd. It's not to much different, what is called diverse, we were taught there is no normal just different . Maybe that's what they are saying now. Right? Right. At 14 I went into a hospital and was officially diagnosed with afhd now prob would b autism then adhd before in a mental ward like my cousin Mary or the Kennedy kid . It's always changing. Some like my great aunt were locked away or like my greatvgrand father who banged his head, like me, trying to shake it all back in, were lucky to have a supportive wife. And now they have a supportive society where you can talk of it or stream of it all. Fir genx we kept our disabilities inside and stayed strong .At least I did ,afraid to let the real me out. I'm finally forgiving myself for having adhd autism and letting her out . What a grand the start of my journey not hiding.

College thoughts of a adhd autism girl

NINE TWELVE NINETY FOUR

My baby brother has long hair which is in a braid. A lot he is almost 12. His birthday is October 19th. He is so cute. His top for his agent, his big feet. His freckles on his face. The ones on his nose are so cute. Most of the time , he can make me laugh no matter what kind of mood i'm in.

9 13 94

I love my mom. I love her because she's so special is the only one that I feel that truly understands me out of all my roads, if she never really made me feel feels stupid when I messed up he would take the time to help me. What also makes her special is that we share so many memories every special I have is that we she features in it all she always been there for me. No matter what I can talk to her about anything in that way. She is more like a friend than a mothermy go to parties in college. I don't have to wonder if I can you tell my mom? I just tell her I can share my interstate with her. You do the reason that I find my mom speci.

9 14 94

My favorite pet I ever had was a cat. We called her Levina. She was a calico cat. We got her when I was in second grade.

She was just a Kitty. She always would go behind the Christmas tree and go to the bathroom. She was a cutest cat I ever had. She had more kittens than ever can be counted. They were the cutest kittens, but none could compare to Lavina. I had her until I was in the fifth grade.

We were going on a car trip and when we were by the ocean in California on a breakshe decided to leave us. We waited and waited. We called her name but she wouldn't come. Finally. After about a 1/2 hour, we decided that she wanted to stay, so we left her by. I'm she was an old cat and probably wanted to die by the ocean. No matter how many cats I have I always he will always be my favorite.

9 15 94

Santa Monica I can see it now I'm walking down the street. I see all the movie theaters I can smell the ocean breeze I can smell it too. It smells and feels so good. I see all the shops I see the restaurant. Johnny Rockets. I also see all the homeless people walking around with carts. I can can see the movie cameras filming a stuff on the beach. I can see the Santa Monica peer with the carouselthe heat is coming down on me and I hear the scene goes floating down the blue sky.9 16 94

The funniest thing that ever happened to someone in my family is when we were driving across country.

It couldn't stop to find a place to Stay the night because of a front jumping contest, it was 11 o'clock at night, and my mom was getting Tired of Driving, We stopped at a hotel, then another and both were full, we thought it had to be a coincidence, but it wasn't after that, we thought a third time my mom asked what was going on. They said there was a frog jumping contest going on who would have crest. All the hotels around for miles were booked. So we ended up driving for half the night. Now, when the story is brought up, we all laugh at the idea. From jumping contest it's just so bar czar it's funny

9 19 o4

I remember learning how to type in eighth grade.

I won the electric typewriter so bad for my birthday, my mom told me that if I won the typewriter that I'd have to learn to type so I signed up for typing at my school. It was hard it took a lot of patients to learn all the keys but eventually it began the master. The art of typing couldn't type fast enough but I did know where the comb keys were and what fingers to use. By time my birthday came, my mom figured out that that I was good enough and I got my typewriter. It came with the typing guide once my class was over. I practiced with that learning to type was hard work, but it was a skill worth learning. I'm glad my mom had me take lessons in eighth grade.

9 20 94

In my wallet, I have some money pictures of friends and family, the theater and movie tickets.A library card And some teenage mutant ninja turtle cards. My brother gave me from this. One could say that family and friend are important to me. I love seeing movies. And plays that I might lot. I enjoy reading that what my brother gives me. I treasure also that I don't have a lot of money.

I 21 94

My most favorite food is my mom's preoggies. She usually makes these once a year, around New Year, she puts potatoes and cheese in them and sometimes cottage ones she makes the dough homemade, the process takes forever, but when they're done, it's all worth it. You can smell them cooking throughout the whole house. They are best with lots of butter and onions.

9 22 94

I love seeing the leaves fall from the trees. I love raking the leaves the smell. The Aeron fall is so cool follows filled with so much. It is halloween thanksgiving my birthday kids starting school football games full of life

9 23 94

In my most comfortable clothes, I wear overalls that have holes in the knees. An extra big T-shirt underneath a pair of Tennis that are really shabby and worn out. Of course, with the baseball cap one backwards. This is me when i'm totally feeling comfortable

9 27 94

The time that I felt closest to nature is when I was in Santa Monica a couple of years ago, it was so great because I was so close to the ocean. Looking out to the water and seeing the water in the sky. Just combine in front of your eye. I felt totally at ease. I really felt as though I was one with nature. Water can do that to me. Any kind of water. But especially ocean water for me is especially healing.

9 28 94

Dear dad, I wish that we could get along better but I don't know how to maybe someday we can be close but right now it is just too hard. This is really hard letter to write, so forgive me if I have a hard time expressing myself. It's just that I feel that I really don't know you're not a stranger but something I feel as if you we were. You may not understand this but I have to write it. I think our worlds are far apart. Do you have anything in common? Besides being father and daughter? Maybe, but right now I can't see it. Perhaps this is because when I was young. I left you and we never really had time to develop a relationship whatever it is I hope. Someday that I will feel comfortable around you. That we can be father and daughter and more than just words saying that you tell people from alicia

9 29 94

My favorite teacher that I ever had was my fourth grade teacher. Her name was miss Pierce. I think she's my favorite teacher because she really understood me. Whatever the case I have fond memories in my fourth grade here. I remember that she had an apple computing. We all played Oregon trail at the end of the year. We had camp out in the room witch was really cool. I remember the book she used to read to us. Books like how to eatfried worms and shell Silverstein books of poems. Whenever I look back to fourth grade, I have to smile. She really made me love school. If it weren't for her, maybe I wouldn't be here charge today. She was a very special teacher.

1. 30 94

It is hard to believe that it is my third year here. It seems like yesterday that I graduated from high school started college. I think I have changed a lot in the last 3 years. I think I'm smarter. Have a better self Esteem and I can trust people better when I look back to who I used to be. It seems I was so young. I can't help but wondering where the time has gone. Time passes so quickly especially when you're not paying strict attention.

1. 3 94

I think that Gandhi's example of non-violence is good.

I think that it shows that you can achieve things without violence, in fact, you probably can achieve more through nonviolence than with violence. I think that when you act do non-violence that you're making more of a point, more people should use this example because if they did, there will be a much happier, not to mention safer place to live. I think most people are afraid to be non-violent because they are worried about. What happened to them? If the other person isn't practicing non-violent ways, I think it is a trust issue. We have to work on people trusting people. Then we can be in a nonviolent society.

10 5 94

My favorite day dream is becoming a Hollywood star. I did dream that I go to Hollywood and working as a waitress, and a big time. Director seized me and he puts me in his newest movie. I've become an important star a riding limos and have a big house plus I win the academy award.

10 6 94

A childhood fear of mine is that I'd be picked last for a team in PE class. I always dreaded playing team sports because it was embarrassing. It is hard waiting to be picked for a team.

Chapters one

Why early intervention works

According to the article early intervention for preschool age children with ADHD, research shows that preschool children with attention-deficit/hyperactivity disorder (ADHD) have a high expulsion rate due to disruptive noncompliant behavior (McGoey, Eckert, & Dupaul, 2002). In preschool, children learn what is expected of them in terms of behavior management. The preschool years are where children learn social skills, structure of classrooms, and pre academic instruction. For the child with ADHD, preschool can be difficult. Early intervention is the key for an ADHD child to be able to have successful preschool years. I will explore the effects of early intervention on preschool children with behavior management issues and a plan will be created that can be used in preschools, to ensure the preschool years go smoothly.

My parents knew I had problems as a child but it was the wonderful sixties or early seventies rather. People wanted to blame behaverial problems children had on life styles.Peple didn't really understand autism , odd or even ADHD then. My parents were left to their own devices. As my mom tells me one doctor said she has problems because you have a guy friend with a earring. Yes that really happened. Can you imagine. I can not. But it is true.

It was not till my teen years that I got the help,I needed. Then maybe it was too late. Oh I survived due to many things. But I often wonder what my life would have been like had I received more. Prom, kisses,boyfriends, friends, better social skills, and the list goes on and on.However there was one thing that saved me.

Theatre and the arts saved me. I found theatre as a child and embraced it head on. I wrote, acted and dreamed of being a Hollywood star. I never became that star , yet any way. Though through the many exercises I did as a actor in my classes and on the different movie sets I have been on I gained a great confidence. Yes indeed. but most important I was saved. I know I sound like a born again christian here. But I am not I am jewish well part , but tht is a whole never book. Anyway arts saved me.

For some it may be sports, science or music but what ever it is let your kids embrace it. I don't know why the arts saved me besides the fact they let me exscape. To a another being with out problems, but I do know that if a child gets early intervention they may not need that escape as much as I did. But I am glad I had it boy am I. The arts saved me and early intervention can save a child you love. I did some many plays and acting classes at pgh playhouse and a b.a in theatre and today's like little women in falcon camp and playing little house with my best friend at ten in ashland . My neighbor. It all gave me purpose. I didn't talk in char Val that much but when I got on stage I was a diff person and completethings , it was all about the art. I couldn't focus or regulate.

Now they know anxiety is all from not regulate.Game changer. Adhd is a regulation and boy that's a game changer right? Amazing. Knowing this now we can help our Littles one and forgive ourselves for not knowing sooner . And keep dreaming .

I dreamed of hollywood. My mansions I would have the husband the kids being famouse and the art . That was my escape my dream my secret garden and not live in anxiety hollywood like life is not a fairy tail but seldom do you get the dream guy hot car and kids or the guy who tracks u down from five states over. No rom coms are not true but they got me through and helped me be happy till I could result on my own.

Chapter two

Why children are getting expelled from preschool

It is a sad thing that children with behaverial problems are not being treated as they should be. In preschool children are being expelled rather then have their problems addressed. Children with behaverial issues are at risk for expulsion from preschool settings due to disruptive and noncompliant behavior (Eckert, Dupaul, & McGoey, 2002)

One needs to ask why Parents do not seem to know that children should be in the least restrictive environment even for preschool. One would think that this would not be the case. There are laws, however that say this and parents seem not to know the facts. Why is this. Well one reason is that the diagnostic and Statistical Manual of Mental Disorders (dsm). The dsm lables adhd , autism and odd but does so in a way that less children can get the help they need. As the dsm changes then more children will get the help they need.The dsm is on the verge of changing. With in the next couple of years this will happen. This will be good for everyone parents, the children and teachers. Why this will be good for everyone is because there are more children in preschool now than ever before, and one out of twenty children have ADHD (Eckert, Dupaul, & Mcgoey, 2002). The fact that more children are in preschool and are at risk creates the need for early intervention in preschool age children. If children can receive the intervention at this critical age there can be fewer problems as the child grows older (www. Kids on the move).The dsm changing helps children by allowing more to get the help need.

Research shows that the earlier the child gets help the better it is for the child.(www.kids on the move) It is in the preschool years that the child is learning who they are and what they need because of this critical time of child development (www. kids on the move). At this age the child is more open to learning, so this is the time that we must help the child (www. kids on the move).

According to child development theories this is the time of childhood to encourage the child and not limit them.

To get the child with ADHD the help they need it may be necessary to up the requirements of teachers in the classroom. To provide quality preschool education for children that have ADHD, we will need educated teachers that know forum ADHD, autism, and odd. Further we will need teachers that know about the range of child development and where the child is and where they should be. By knowing child development theories this can decrease the expele rate of children with behaverial issues.

Chapter three

Children with behavioral problems are being expelled at an alarming rate from their preschool classrooms. There is not enough early intervention in the preschool years when a child is developing. When one out of twenty children has ADHD, this is a problem. Help cannot wait until early elementary school years. Further when a child does get help in the elementry school years it comes in the form of an individual education plan (i.e.p.) and/or medication. I have seen that when a child waits to get help even in elementry schools it may already be to late. Children are already building up anxiety and developing self-esteem problems. With early intervention in the preschool years there is a great developmental opportunity possible here.

The primary goal of early internvetion is to explore the role early intervention plays in the preschool class room in terms of behavior management. Recommendations can be made for the teacher regarding the need for affective interventions in early childhood. When one has a child with behavior issues one should investigate interventions that will help the child improve and suceed in preschool and beyond. Recommendations will be made to bring about change in the preschool classbeyondnd home to improve conditions for the children, parents and teachers.

chapter Four

Early intervention for preschool kids with behavioral problems

To bring about this change three things will be looked at.First it will be looked at what the developmental issues facing preschool children in terms of behavior management issues are.Second it will be explored what ways early intervention help the child with behavior management issues develop better.Lastly it will be explored what is the best way to approach early intervention in the preschool classroom for the child with behavior issues.This chapter will provide information that will be beneficial for teachers, social workers, admin, therapists, teacher aids, and parents and or caregivers that come in contact with children of preschool age, that have behavior issues. Increased awareness for early intervention is pivotal for the future of the field and the child.

This chapter will focus on behavaral issues in preschool kids and why early intervention is important. Included in the will be an over view of child development for the preschool years, current definitions of ADHD, odd and autism, how preschools handle disabilities, the diagnosis from the dianostiuac symptom manual (DSM) and what interventions work for preschool children.

A child in the preschool years of development is at a time in their development where there brain is expanding and growing rapidly. It is at this time of their development that children are exploring their world. At the age of three the child's mind is going through a very strong development. It is at this stage that children are beginning to learn that everything is not what it seems (Robinson, 2008).

Children are beginning to play pretend and fantasy play (Robinson, 2008). Children are still learning what is real and what not real (Robinson, 2008). During this time in life a child is learning what they want to do. Children are learning and developing their own view of the world from their experiences in life (Robinson, 2008). So it is at this age that children learn both the positive and negative experiences they carry with them. At this age it is important to bring about positive experiences for the child and encourage them to grow. A child should have the encouragement to explore the world and have new experiences. A child needs to learn who they are.

The preschool child is not just learning about academics in preschool. In preschool the three year old is learning how to act, learning right from wrong, how to get along with others, sharing and how to pay attention. Everything they bring to preschool is what they have learned from caregivers and from the perspectives from what they have seen thus far (Robinson, 2008).

It is in these years that a child is very egotistical. They are going through a phase in their life that they think about themselves. This is because they are beginning to explore their world and very focused on themselves. This is due to the child just beginning to learn themselves and their interests. A child is getting better at many activities.

Children at the age of three blend colors and they draw shapes on shapes and draw carefree (Robinson, 2008). Children are beginning to think about what they draw and take it very seriously (Robinson, 2008). Children are beginning to understand what comes next in events. . chapter five

An overview of child development

Scemas

Language

Emotions

Play

Dramatic play

. Fine motor skills

Schemas

When it comes to ADHD there are many problems for a teacher to recognize. First the child with ADHD may have trouble with schemas (Hallowell,& Ratey, 2005, pg.6). Having trouble with schemas causes many problems. One of the many problems caused is the child does not understand the time or sequence it takes to do things. For instance in school if the child is doing an art project they may think they have time and will get caught up talking to a friend, spend time putting away toys and getting the supplies and then be surprised or upset when they do not finish the project.

Children are learning about schemas in preschool (Piaget, 1972, pg. 57). If the child has a link the child learns better. For example if child has a marbles they may not learn the concept of fewer or the sequence of events. However if the child learns with chocolates they know what is more or less. Though this can vary at times.

It is important to remember that children are just beginning to be concrete in their thinking. When working with children teachers need to broaden what children already know and broaden their perspective. By realizing the development level the child is at children can learn more. Further you as a parent will not get as frustrated.

Language

By the age of three to four the preschool child should know 1,0000 to 1,500 words (Hobday&Ollier,1999,pg. 5)Children at this age will be able to understand and comprehend(Hobday & Ollier, 1999 pg. 5) Also children will use words more than temper tantrums at this age (Hobday & Ollier, 1999 pg. 5).

Emotions

At the age of three children will know sad, mad and angry (Hobday & Ollier, 1999 pg. 5).

Though you may have to give examples and remind the children what the emotions mean. Children will need reminders because they are just beginning to develop

Play

At the age of three children are beginning to parallel play (Weininger, 1979,pg.34). Parallel play is when children play next to each other, but not with each other. For example in parallel play two children will play next to each other in the sand box digging and making their own castles. They will not acknowledge the other child. Play is a very important part of this time of life for the child. One can learn a lot from how a child plays because the child is learning to assimilate (Bergen, 1986, pg. 52).

Dramatic Play

A good way to learn about the child and their stage of development is to watch them in dramatic play using their imagination (Piaget, 1972, pg. 57). According to Piaget the child is in the sub period of preparatory representations (Piaget, 1972, pg. 57.). An example of this stage is the child who is playing dress up and house. The child now can use items in the way they were meant to be used.

Bilateral development

By the age of three the child will have good Bilateral Development (Hooper, 1998, pg.118). The child will be able to use scissors, and use both hands to do activities (Hooper, 1998, pg. 118). The child further will be able to control their movements.

Fine motor skills

At the age of three the child should be able to have the skill to shift (Hopper, 1998, pg. 121). An example of fine motor skills would be when the child is drawing with a crayon and beginning to be able to control their movement and move their hand to the tip of the crayon.

In order to teach children and notice problems children may have, a good way to teach is naturalistically (Diamond, Hestenes & O'Conner, 1994)). By teaching a child naturally one can teach the children from the developmental level the child is at. Further the teacher is teaching from the moment and using the moments of the children to teach. By teaching the child from the child's developmental level the teacher can catch issues that may arise.

Chapter six

History of disabilities in preschool

In preschools for children with disabilities not much has changed, but preschoclassrooms have (Fletcher& Satz, 1988). One out of twenty children has ADHD and one in six classrooms will have a child that has a disability (Fletcher & Satz, 1988). More often than not a preschool child with a behavioral disability is expelled from the preschool classroom (Hillside, 2011). It is not acceptable to expel the child that has a disability, rather than help the child.

A tool that preschool teachers have to help a child with disabilities is a screening (Ireton, 1984). A screening is a short reliable way of seeing if a child has a disability. A screening is not a diagnosis. A screening will only tell where the child is at developmentally (Ireton, 1984). If a child is seen from the screening to have a developmental problem, it should be recommended to get a pediatrician (Ireton, 1984).

A pediatrician can do an evaluation and get a diagnosis (Ireton, 1984). The doctors' evaluation will provide more detailed information about the child's abilities. The parents then have decisions to make about the child's education.

Rather than expel the child with a disability, there are two ways to help the child.

The first way is when the child is a few months from three years old the parents should contact their local school (Mauro, 2011). School districts have a special education department where a child with disabilities can receive the help they need (Mauro, 2011). In special education preschools classes are shorter and the children all have disabilities (Mauro, 2011).

The second way to help a child with disabilities is an inclusion preschool (Diamond, 1994). Inclusion preschools have children with and without disabilities. When children are in inclusion preschools children learn more. Children without disabilities can become more sensitive in nature (Diamond, 1994). Children with disabilities benefit from inclusion preschools because they become more social and their behavior problems can become less (Diamond, 1994).

Both special education and inclusion preschools have their benefits. Parents need to look at the law before they decide what type of program is best for their child. The law clearly states that the child should be in the least restrictive environment.

Federal law

Several federal laws exist in the United States entitling every student to a free and appreciate education (fape) in the least restrictive environment (lre). The laws allow for the adaptations, accommodations and modifications to enable students to participate and learn in general education. In addition to those laws each state has their own rules and laws that must be upheld.

Law PL94- 142 insures that children can learn in the least restrictive environment (Thurman & Wilderstrom, 1990 pg. 29). While the law PL 99- 457 ensures that preschool children receive early intervention in an integrated setting (Thruman & Wilderstrom, 1990, pg. 29).Research shows that children with handicaps of any kind benefit from being in a class with others without disabilities (Thruman & Wilderstrom, 1990, pg. 29.)

The American with disability act (ada) is a federal law prohibiting discrimination in programs, services and access by state and local government agencies. The intervals with disabilities act (IDEA) of 1997 is designed to provide federal assistance to state and local education agencies in order to guarantee special education and related services to eligible children with disabilities(Bowe, 2000 pg. 40).

In preschool education, the law in section 619 of part b mandates that all preschools serve preschool children with disabilities, in a law from 1986 (Bowe, 2000 pg. 40). Section 504 of the rehabilitant act of 1973 is a law prohibiting discrimination on the bias of ones disability in programs and activities receiving federal finical assistance(Melikyan, 2006).

A parent or teacher can request an evaluation to determine whether the child is qualified for services under the idea or section 504 (Melikyan, 2006). If the child is found to qualify at the preschool level they can be set up in a special education preschool or the less restricted environment needed. To help parents who may be overwhelmed by all of this there is CHADD.

The group children and adults with ADHD (CHADD) is good for advocacy (Hallowell & Ratey, 2005, pg. 355). CHADD is a support group for parents and children and adults. CHADD is focused on three ideas,1) promoting scientific research for ADHD, access to evidence based treatment and interventions from diverse populations with ADHD, and 3) protecting and, enhancing, safe guards while improving and reducing discrimination so that all with ADHD get the help they need.

Chaphelps seven

Issues of gender:

why gender is a issue with children with behavior issues?

Research has shown that boys with ADHD are diagnosed more often than girls with ADHD (Carta, 2006, pg. 35).

Research is beginning to show however that just as many girls have ADHD as boys, but are being over looked in terms of diagnoses (Carta, 2006, pg. 35). The problem in diagnosing girls is they do not have the same hyperactive symptoms as do boys (Carta, 2006, pg. 35). Girls can be seen as day dreamers and just not interested in academics in general (Carta, 2006, pg.35). Teachers tend to do less evals on girls, even when the symptoms are the same as boys (Carta, 2006, pg.36).

The later a girl gets diagnosed the more problems they can have (Carta, 2006, pg.36). Without early intervention both boys and girls can suffer from emotional problems (Carta, 2006, pg 36). It is important to do early intervention on both girls and boys and to know what to look for when it comes to ADHD.

Chapter eight

ADHD problems:

What parents and teachers need to look for

The child with ADHD may have behavioral problems and a mix of opposition deficit disorder(ODD), a disorder with extreme behavior problems. ODD is often found with ADHD (American psychiatric association, 2005, pg. 93). ODD and ADHD together cause many extreme problems behaviorally (American psychiatric association, 2005 pg. 93). Having behavioral problems due to ADHD and ODD may manifest itself in being hyper and cause acting out. The hyper child can pay less attention and move about the class more, which can lead to social skills problems.

Another symptom of ADHD,odd and autism is, social skills problems (Haalloowell & Ratey, 2005, pg.265). When the child has behavioral management issues this can cause other children not to want to be around the child. The teacher dealing with the child that has these issues may be challenged by the student due to the child's problems and not know what to do.

It may be hard to see if there is a disability. To see if there is a disability one must take into account that lack of attention, impulsivity, lack of schemas, problem with social skills, and behavioral problems all have to be extreme. (Kaiser& Raminsky,199, pg.7). All kids have lack of attention, problem social skills or behavior problems (Kaiser & Rasminsky, 1999, pg. 7). However, by the age of three however must children are learning not to be aggressive, but to use their words (Kaiser & Rasminsky, 199, pg. 9). For the child with ADHD their symptoms show in good and bad moments, not just bad moments and must be extreme (Hillside, 2011).

If the child with ADHD,autism, or odd is to be helped then there has to be early intervention. Early intervention helps the child's symptoms be less and better managed (Hillside, 2011). Early intervention helps the child learn social skills, behavior management and to have better attention.

A naturalistic way of teaching can help achieve the goals of better social skills and behavior management (Diamond, Hestenes & O'Conner, 1994).Further by using child development theories you can understand where the child with disabilities is at. This can help educate the child and diagianoise the child.

Behaverial issues are hard to diagnose in preschool however it can be done. While the DSM only looks at school age children that is changing. In future additions there will be a broader age range for children with ADHD (Hillside, 2011). By the dsm providing a broader age rage for children starting in preschool this will help provide early interventions in preschool age children .

As in ADHD I think the changes in autism and odd will only give people a greater understanding of what they are. I believe this to be the case because when ever something is discussed people understand more what something is. In this case some people think that autism and odd can be limited , however from my undesanding it is Broading the diangois after then limiting it so more services can be offered. Which can only be a good idea for families with children with thze disorders.

chapter Nine

Definition of ADHD and Autism and Odd

For a child to have ADHD they have to, have a persistent pattern of inattention and hyper impulsivity and be more severe than it would be in one without ADHD. ADHD is a disorder in which children are significantly limited in their ability to filter out irreverent input, focus, organize, prioritize, delay gratification, think before they act or perform other executive functions that must of us perform automatically(Reiff, 2004, pg 3). If ADHD can be looked at and understand in the preschool years and an early intervention set up during these years the child may have else issues as an adult (Reiff, 2004 pg.3).

DSM diagnosis criteria for ADHD 314.01

Either one or two

Six or more of the following symptoms of inattention have persisted for a t least 6 months to a degree that is maladaptive and inconsistent with the development level. :

Inattention

A. Often fails to give close attention to details or makes careless mistakes in schoolwork, work or other activities
B. Often has difficulty sustaining attention in tasks or play activates
C. Often does not seem to listen when spoken to directly.

d. Often does not follow through on instructions and fails to finish schoolwork, chores, or duties, in the work place (not due to oppositional behavior or failure to understand instructions). E. Often has difficulty organizing tasks and activities.

A. Often avoids, dislikes or is relevant to engage in tasks that require sustained mental effort

B. Often loses things necessary for tasks.
C. Easily distracted by extraneous stimuli.
D. Is often forgetful in daily activities

2. Six or more of the following symptoms are of hyperactivity impulsivity having persisted for at least six months to a degree that is maladaptive and inconsistent with developmental level.

Hyperactivity:

A. Often fidgets with hands or feet or squirms in seat
B. Often leaves seat in classroom or other situations in which remaining seated is expected
C. Often runs about or climbs excessively in situations that are inappropriate.
D. Often has difficulty playing or engaging in leisure activity quietly
E. often seems on the go or often acts as if driven by a motor
F. Often talks excessively

Impulsivity

A. Often blurts out answers before questions have been completed
B. Often has difficulty waiting turns
C. Often interrupt or intrudes on others (buts into conversations or games) (American psychiatric association, 2005, pg. 78 to 85)

Definition of oppositional defiant disorder.

The essential feature of ODD is a recurrent pattern of negative, deficient, dissident and hostile behavior toward authority. When a preschool child acts out one should look at the below features to see if the child has the disorder. For the preschool child the symptoms have to be extreme to be considered for the disorder.

DSM diagnose for oppositional deficit disorder (odd) 313.81

A pattern of negative, defiant and hostile, behavior lasting 6 months during which four or more of the following are present: 1. Often loses temper

1. Often argues with adults
2. Often actively defies or refuses to comply with adult's requests or rules
3. Often deliberately annoys people
4. Often blames others for his or her mistakes or misbehavior
5. Is often touchy or easily annoyed by others
6. Is often angry and resentful
7. Is often spiteful or vindictive

A. The disturbance in behavior causes clinically significant impairment in social academic or occupational functioning.
B. The behaviors do not occur during a mood disorder
C. Criteria does not met the requirements for conduct disorder and if over 18 does not met requirements for antisocial personality disorder.(American psychiatric association, 2005, pg. 91 to 93

299.00 Autistic criteria for autistic disorder

The patient fulfills a total of at least six criteria from the following here lists:

Impaired social interaction:(at least two)

Defict regulation of social interaction due to bad eye contact, facial expressions,body posture and gestures,

Lack of peer relationships that are reveals to age grouping and development,

Apsence of wanting to share achievements,interests or pleasure with others,

Apsence of social or emotional reciprocity

Impaired communicatired on at least one:

Delayed or absent development of spoken language of which the child does not comphensate with gestures

In patients who can speak noticable defictancy in ability to begin or substation a conversation

Language that is repetive, stereo typed or idosyncratic

Approcriate to developmental stage , absence of social imitative play or spontaneous make believe play

Activties and intrests that are repetitive ,restricted, stereotyped(at least one):

Abnormal fascination with and preoccuption with interests that are restricted and stereotyped such as spinning things.

Rigid performance of routines or rituals that do not seem to have a function

Repetitive stereotyped motor mannerisms such as hand flapping

Persistant observation with parts of objects

Before the age of three patient shows delayed or abnormal functioning in one or mo of the following areas:

Imaginative or symbolic play

Social interaction

Language used in social interaction

It should be noted these symptoms are further not better explained by Rett's disorder or childhood Chapter14

Early intervention in preschool:

Ways to help children with behavior problems in the classroom

So now what?Now that we know what ADHD, autism an odd is how do we help your beloved that suffers from these disorders. Well have no fear. There are several different ways to help the child.

Naturalistic teaching

For ADHD children in preschool a good intervention is a naturalistic approach to teaching (Diamond, Hestenes, & O'Conner, 1994).

The naturalistic approach to teaching is good way to teach all children, because it deals with the problems in the moment it occurs (Diamond, Hestenes, & O'Conner, 1994). For instance you are in the classroom and a child talks out of turn you can take that opportunity to tell the child that it is better to wait their turn and raise their hand.

A child with ADHD according to the DSM "will not be able to sit still". While all preschool children are just learning the rules of class, a child without disabilities will understand this sooner and stop the inappropriate behavior (Diamond, Hestenes & O'Conner, 1994). By using the naturalistic style of teaching as an intervention the child learns what is appropriate and other children also get a lesson. Preschool is about learning what is expected and the naturalistic approach of teaching as intervention helps all children learn the rules (Diamond, Hestenes & O' Conner, 1994).

Dramatic Play

As I mentioned earlier play is a big idea in pre school. Play can help the children with behavior issues and should be used as a intervention.Play is an intervention for children with ADHD because play serves as an assimilative tool (Bergen, 1986, pg. 52). What may look like just play is so much more. Children need play to learn what society expects from them (Bergen, 1986, pg.52). Dramatic play is a good way for a teacher to learn where the child is developmentally. By watching children with behaverial issuesplay one will be able to understand better the child is at developmentaly.

One can learn from the child in play many ways. One way to help the child learn through play is to do activities with the children. For instance to help children learn about feelings you can do a face mask (Hobday & Ollier, 1999, pg.27). The aim of the face mask is to help children learn that people cover up feelings (Hobday & Ollier, 1999, pg. 27).

The second way to help children through play is in dramatic play (Bergen, 1988, pg. pg.17). Since the child is just using their imagination one can watch the child in the dress up area or in story time. Children will be pretending with replica items such as miniature items of real items such as cars, houses or people (Bergen, 1988). Play as an intervention is a very good way to help children.

According to Neumann when a child is in dramatic play teachers must judge whether the child a) has a degree of control over the play situation, b) determines the degree of reality the child has, and c) provides motivation for the activity (Bergen, 1988, pg.19).

Activity Based Intervention

Secondly is activly based intervention. In using an activity based intervention the teacher considers where the child developmentally and how their goals can be included in the classroom (Diamond, 1994).

For instance with the child with ADHD if the child has trouble sitting still you can do activities that help the child learn to sit still. An example would be story telling. In storytelling time the child needs to sit still. The teacher can tell the child what do we do during story time...we sit still. An activity based intervention helps the child learn and lets the teacher teach in the moment.

If a teacher gets the necessary training to help the child with ADHD, Odd, or Autism behavior problems, the classroom experience can be better for the child and the child's peers. Further if the child gets early intervention there will be fewer problems in later years. The different methods of early intervention are important for anyone dealing with young children to know, so that the child does not develop low self-esteem or behavior problems. When ADHD, autism or odd is found in preschool children and an early intervention is done, in later years the child or adult, may not have to go through social skills training or behavior management training because the positive effects of preschool are evident (Joseph & Strain, 2003).Not needing social skills training is good for you because this means you do not have as many issues to carry with you through out your life.

Chapter ten

Classssroom management techniques teachers or parents can use to help a child with Behavior issues to help the teacher help the child.

So now that we have the intentions, what next?Well how does a teacher or parent approach the child with behavioral management issues due to behavior issues.Well their are several strategies used in preschool settings to work with children with behavioral problems due to ADHD, Autism or Odd.

First off the number one strategerie is understand the child. This does not mean baby the child or give them everything they want.You need to create a plan to help the parents understand what is going on and to heLp guide the child. Again you may be asking how do I do this.

Well if you have the a child in your classroom you may want to do surveys. Surveys create paper work that helps you better understand your subject.In a survey you can create questions that will let you examine, what is going on for your child in the classroom and to see where's they are at developmentally. This will give you better clues to what your child needs. Then you can take that survey and the information you found back to the parents and the child is better understood. By creating surverys you are developing a plan and using qualative research.

By using Qualitative research to help children with behavioral issues one is exploring the indivual child.Qualative researce is designed to understand selected issues in depth and detail. It allows the research to take place without being bound by predetermined categories of analysis. The methodologies such as gathering responses to open ended questions enable the researcher to understand and capture the points of view of other people, thereby elucidating their understanding of the world. Whereas quantitative research makes it possible to measure major patterns through statistical data, qualitative data inquiry provides depth, detail and individual meaning for studying a limited number of case studies.This is why children with behavialal issues can be helped more. In looking at my story and using qualitive research I could get more help.

If you remember I created my case study early on. You may want to go back to chapter one and refresh your memory. That said case studys help because you are identifying what is wrong with the person you are trying to help. A case study is one of many tools you can use to help the child in your class room.

Another such tool that can be used is the interview to help a child. A interview is a one on one setting where you have access to your subject. Having one on one access. Gets you to help your child even more.

Secondly is observation. By watching the group of people that you are researching when you are not in the picture you are giving the child the freedom to be themselves. By giving the child freedom to be themselves you are letting them explore and hence the real child comes out. You get to find out what can help the child. Further you can compare the child with the disability to other children . One gets to see everyone in a sitition. This could make it easier to determine if there is issues with the particular child in question.

Lastly is reflective journaling. This is writing about your experiences. By writing about your experiences you are keeping track of what makes the child do something and hence you are creating a better view of the child. Futher you have something to back you up when you talk to the parents. Also in your reflective journaling it may be good to use research you found on the subject and use that to further help your child so that parents know they are not alone.

I go back to how I started this section.One has to understand their child.The things I listed are for teachers and parents. You can use observation, naturalistic teaching, play, case study, reflective journaling and surveys as a parent. To create a plan you need to know where your child devlopmentally is at, that is the most important thing.Understanding child development can only give you a clue to what your child needs.It opens up a great way to understand your child and what they need and a great way to start a plan for your child.

Epilogue

When all is said and done you are the one that can help your child.

Every child needs some person to realize they can do it. My mother, was that person for me. My mother was very influenceual with helping me and guding me. Everyone with a disability needs that one person that encourages them to suceed. Be that champion for your child. They will thank you. It may be exhausting but well worth it. I hope this book has opened you up and shown you a step by step by step method and or guide to helping your child succed. I have included the references for further reading and or tools to use. Lastly have faith that you know your child. I am now thirty eight years old. I wont lie. It is a constant struggle still for me but i am the eprson i am because i recieved encouragement. I went to college. I am getting my grad degree and hope to be married and maybe even have kids. I am a adult with adhd and behavior issues. I was that kid everyone looked at weirdly but I know that adult that can use that to their advantage. Have faith you will come out of this alive my mother did and you and your child will too. It is tough being different but you can do for your child. Remember that as hard as it is on you it is even harder on ghe child. Dont give up on them.

Lastly if you are adult with this disorder reading this book. I think it can help you. Use it as a tool. Children today have more researches then we did. It is seen more that a child has a disability. Talked about more. Though in my opinion just because it is talked about more does not make it any easier. Sometimes it can be harder to have a disability beause now everyone knows you have a disability. I was diagnoised as a teen. This is when you dont want to be different. I fought and it and got worse before I got better. I had a mixture of odd, autism , ADHD, seizes and learning disabilties. Through my writings you can see who I wanted to be. I never could quite get there as a teen. Though a child diagnosed today as a young preschooler. They can go to prom, have a girlfriend, or boyfriend, be sweet sixteen and more. They no longer have to wonder what it is like...what if. So take this book to heart and get that preschool child the early intervention they need. Further if you are the adult with a behaverial problem like me,just remember we helped these children be stronger by telling our stories.Lets continue doing soon. Good luck to all on their journeys.

The years fly by (1992)

It seems to me just a wee bit ago I was nothing but a tot,Now I'm 17,trying to rid myself of the hands that reach out to me as I fall,But now unlike then I don't want the hands.

References

Bowe.F. (2004). Early Childhood Education Birth to Eight. Delmer Learning New York New

York

Bergen.D. (1988) Play as a medium for learning and Development A handbook of Theory and Practice. Heinmann, New Hampshire.

Carta J.(2006) My daughters Journey: A Child with ADHD and Asperger's Syndrome Navigates The School System. Pasadena Ca, Pacific Oaks.

Diagnostic And Statistical Manual Of Mental Disorders (2009) DSM. American Psychiatric Association, Arlington, Va.

Diamond.K. (1994) Integrating Children with Disabilities into preschool. Eric Digest.

Eye.A., Gremillion.M., Martel.M.,Nigg. J., Roberts.B. (2010). The structure of Childhood Disruptive Behaviors. Psychological Assessment vol. 22 no.4 816- 826.

Fletcher. J., Satz.P.(1988). Early Identification of Learning Disabled Children: A old Problem Revisited. Journal of Consulting and Clinical Psychology. No. 6 824- 826.

Ireton.H., Lichtenstein.R.(1984). Preschool Screening: Identifying young Children With Developmental Problems. Professional School Of Psychology 309- 311.

Kaiser.B., Rasminsky.J. (1999). Meeting the Challenge. Effective Strategies for Challenging Behaviors in Early Childhood Environments. Canadian Childcare Federation, Ontario.

Hallowell.E.Ratey.J. (2005).Delivered From Distraction Getting The Most out Of Life with Attention Deficit Disorder. Ballantine Books, New York.

Hobday.A., Ollier.K.(1999). Creative Therapy with Adolescents. Impact, California.

Hooper.S., Umansky .W. (1998)Young Children With Special Needs. Prentice Hall, New Jersey.

Humphrey.J. (1990).Helping Learning Disabled Gifted Children learn Through Compensatory Active Play. Charles S. Thompson, Illinois

Melikyan.S. (2006).Adult Children with Attention DeficitHyperactivity Disorder (ADHD) A Tool For Parents. Pacific Oaks, California.

Mauro.T. (2011). Early Intervention To Special Needs Education Pre K.

Robinson.M. (2008).Child Development from Birth to Eight: A Journey through the Early Years.

Open University Press,

Piaget.J. (1973).The Child Problems and Genetic Psychology Reality. Grossman, New York.

Weinninger.O.(1979).Play and Education The Basic tool for Learning. Charles C Thomas, Illinois.